The BLUE JEAN JACKET

How Abandonment Affects Your Health, Wealth, and Relationships

REFLECTION JOURNAL

Rena Perozich

The Blue Jean Jacket Reflection Journal
How Abandonment Affects Your Health, Wealth, and Relationships
By Dr. Rena Perozich

ISBN: 979-8-9992217-6-6

Prepared for Publication By

PUBLISHING

MAKING YOUR BOOK A REALITY

Cedar Point, NC | 843-929-8768 | info@BandBpublishingLLC.com

DISCLAIMER

This reflection journal accompanies The Blue Jean Jacket book, which is a personal memoir and reflects the author's individual experiences, perspectives, and recollections. It is not intended to diagnose, treat, or provide medical or psychological advice or counseling. Readers are encouraged to seek the guidance of qualified health professionals regarding any physical, mental, or emotional health concerns. Any actions taken based on the content of this book are solely at the reader's discretion and risk.

TO CONTACT THE AUTHOR
renaperozich.com

CONTENTS

CHAPTER ONE..5
The Epiphany

CHAPTER TWO 13
No One Likes You

CHAPTER THREE 21
Sleepless Nights

CHAPTER FOUR 29
Self-Sabotaging Behaviors and Coping Skills

CHAPTER FIVE..37
Ignoring Appetites and Bodily Functions

CHAPTER SIX..45
How Abandonment Affects Health

CHAPTER SEVEN 55
How Abandonment Affects Wealth

CHAPTER EIGHT..65
How Abandonment Affects Relationships

CHAPTER NINE 73
The Fear of Loss and Disappointments

CHAPTER TEN 81
The Fear of Intimacy

CHAPTER ELEVEN 89
Dissociation

CHAPTER TWELVE 97
Wearing a New Jacket

ABOUT THE AUTHOR..103
Dr. Rena Perozich

PAUSE

This Reflection Journal is designed to accompany *THE BLUE JEAN JACKET* by Rena Perozich. If you're holding this journal but haven't yet read the book—pause right here. The journey begins with The Blue Jean Jacket. Visit ***renaperozich.com*** to order your copy and step fully into the story that sets the stage for your healing and reflection.

A NOTE TO THE READER

Although I have been involved in pastoral ministry and Christian pastoral counseling for many, many years, I am not a licensed mental health counselor, therapist, or medical professional, and this book should not be used as a substitute for professional support or treatment.

The experiences described in *The Blue Jean Jacket* book and any reference to them in this *Reflection Journal* are drawn from my own life. I have researched this subject extensively, and I present this material as a lay person who has experienced the effects of childhood abandonment and childhood emotional neglect and found a path toward healing.

Because my studies have spanned more than a decade and literally include dozens of authors, podcasters, articles, journals, and videos, it is impossible for me to remember and give appropriate credit to every thought. When you study a subject over time—particularly one that has captured your interest but you never considered writing about—the information becomes part of you. It becomes hard to remember where you learned what and from whom. I have done my best to give honor where honor is due and worked diligently to cite my sources. I have also provided an extensive bibliotherapy at the back of *The Blue Jean Jacket* book to encourage further study by the reader.

CHAPTER ONE

The Epiphany

CHAPTER SUMMARY

Chapter One begins with a seemingly simple crisis-misplacing a beloved blue jean jacket-that spirals into a deep emotional episode. As Dr. Rena Perozich frantically searches for the jacket before a long road trip to support a grieving friend, the panic she experiences reveals far more than a lost item. Her intense emotional attachment to the jacket uncovers unresolved trauma from childhood abandonment and neglect.

Throughout the chapter, Dr. Perozich shares how the jacket had become her companion, a source of comfort and consistency in an otherwise unstable life. Losing it triggered dissociation and anxiety, which she later recognizes as rooted in unhealed wounds from her past. Through the lens of trauma theory, she reflects on the power of emotional attachment to objects when human relationships have failed to provide security. The eventual rediscovery of the jacket at home-hiding in plain sight-becomes symbolic of the hidden emotional truths she must confront.

The chapter ends with an awakening: the realization that her attachment to the jacket masked deeper emotional pain. This moment marks the beginning of her journey toward healing and invites readers to reflect on their own unacknowledged wounds.

KEY THEMES AND INSIGHTS

- **Trauma response**: Panic, dissociation, and emotional regression in the face of a minor loss reflect deeper unresolved trauma.

- **Attachment to objects**: The jacket symbolizes a sense of control, comfort, and protection that the author lacked in her early life.

- **Abandonment issues**: The loss of the jacket reactivates fears of abandonment and worthlessness rooted in childhood neglect.

- **Healing awareness**: Recognizing the jacket as a stand-in for emotional security becomes the "epiphany" that opens the door to self-exploration.

JOURNAL QUESTIONS

1. Have you ever felt an intense attachment to a specific object? What meaning does it hold for you?

2. When was the last time you experienced panic or anxiety over something small? Could it have been a trigger for something deeper?

3. What early life experiences might have shaped your emotional responses to loss or abandonment?

4. Have you ever dissociated-felt emotionally numb or detached-during a stressful moment? What do you think your mind was protecting you from?

5. What "epiphanies" have you had about your past that shifted how you see yourself today?

6. Do you allow yourself to grieve small losses, or do you dismiss them as insignificant? Why might both big and small losses matter?

7. In what ways have you sought comfort or safety outside of relationships-with routines, habits, or objects?

8. Are there any "chapters" in your life you've closed too quickly, without fully understanding what they meant to you?

9. What are you grateful for today?

10. What is one action you can take today to show greater awareness, presence, or intention toward a healthier mindset?

CHAPTER TWO

No One Likes You

CHAPTER SUMMARY

This chapter is a raw, emotional reflection on abandonment, shame, and the development of a performative identity in response to childhood trauma. The author recounts the day her mother left without warning, leaving behind a note and her wedding rings. This event marked the beginning of a life driven by survival, responsibility, and perfectionism.

As the oldest of five children, the narrator stepped into a caregiving role, raising her siblings and taking on adult responsibilities well before her time. To cope, she became a "performer"— constantly seeking approval through excellence, afraid of showing vulnerability or truth. This coping mechanism left her emotionally exhausted and disconnected from her true self.

The chapter also explores the generational impact of dysfunction, addiction, and silence. The author unpacks the shame instilled by an alcoholic parent and how it led to chronic feelings of unworthiness, anxiety, and self-doubt. She ultimately identifies her experience as a form of PTSD, caused by emotional abandonment and neglect.

Despite its heaviness, the chapter ends with a message of healing and solidarity: you are not alone in your pain, and there is a path through the wounds to hope and wholeness.

KEY THEMES & INSIGHTS

- **Abandonment Trauma:** Sudden parental abandonment and its long-term emotional consequences.

- **Performing for Acceptance:** How children become perfectionists to earn love and prevent further loss.

- **Shame and Silence:** The insidious nature of shame that thrives in secrecy and fear.

- **Parentification:** The role reversal where children take on adult responsibilities too early.

- **Emotional Legacy of Addiction:** How a parent's addiction shapes the self-worth and identity of a child.

- **The Illusion of Control:** Believing that being "good enough" can prevent pain or abandonment.

- **Path to Healing:** Acknowledging trauma as a shared human experience and beginning the journey to healing.

JOURNAL QUESTIONS

1. What parts of this chapter resonated most deeply with your own experiences? Why?

2. Have you ever found yourself "performing" or striving for perfection to gain love or acceptance? What did that cost you emotionally?

3. Think about a time when you felt abandoned (emotionally or physically). How did that moment shape the way you view yourself or others?

4. The author mentions shame as a constant companion. How has shame shown up in your life, and how do you respond to it?

5. What messages or "scripts" did you learn as a child that still influence your decisions today? Are they helpful or harmful?

6. How do you typically cope with the fear of being left or rejected? What are healthier ways you could respond to that fear?

7. Reflect on the concept that 'shame that binds us can also blind us.' What might shame be preventing you from seeing clearly in your own life?

8. What does healing look like for you? Are there small steps you could take today toward that healing?

9. Who in your life today makes you feel emotionally safe? How can you cultivate more of those relationships?

10. What would it mean for you to stop performing and be your authentic self? What fears come up, and what freedom might that offer?

11. What are you grateful for today?

12. What is one action you can take today to show greater awareness, presence, or intention toward a healthier mindset?

C H A P T E R   T H R E E

Sleepless Nights

CHAPTER SUMMARY

In this powerful and deeply vulnerable chapter, the author explores how childhood abandonment and trauma shaped her adult life—particularly her ability to rest, trust, and feel safe. She recounts experiences of emotional neglect, the absence of maternal affection, and taking on adult responsibilities far too young. Her mother's emotional unavailability and eventual departure left deep scars that disrupted the author's sense of security and self-worth.

The chapter vividly describes how these early wounds manifested in adulthood through insomnia, nightmares, trust issues, hyper-independence, and self-sabotage. She shares a chilling memory of a man emerging from her attic—an unresolved trauma that contributed to her lifelong struggle with sleep and anxiety.

By seeking medical help, engaging in therapy, spiritual practices, and building consistent sleep routines, the author slowly begins to find healing. She emphasizes the importance of asking for help, the value of self-understanding, and the power of facing long-buried pain. While healing is hard work, it is possible—and worth it.

KEY THEMES & INSIGHTS

- **Emotional Abandonment:** Even before her mother physically left, the emotional absence had already created a deep sense of being unseen, unloved, and unimportant.

- **Sleep and Trauma:** Sleep disorders, insomnia, and nightmares are shown as symptoms of childhood trauma and PTSD.

- **Hyper-Independence:** Growing up too fast can lead to the belief that asking for help is weakness.

- **Trust and Intimacy Struggles:** Fear of vulnerability creates barriers in relationships, even safe ones.

- **False Beliefs (Ungodly Beliefs):** Replacing harmful inner scripts with truth-based beliefs is crucial.

- **The Body Keeps Score:** The body holds trauma, even when the mind does not recall the details.

- **The Power of Help:** Healing starts by asking for and accepting support. It's strength, not weakness.

JOURNAL QUESTIONS

1. When do you feel most unseen or unheard? How do you typically respond in those moments?

2. Have you ever told yourself, "I have to handle this on my own"? Where do you think that belief came from?

3. Reflect on your earliest memories of bedtime. Were they peaceful or anxiety-filled? How does sleep feel for you now?

4. What do your dreams or recurring thoughts at night reveal about unresolved fears or emotions?

5. What are some "ungodly beliefs" or harmful inner scripts you've carried from childhood? How might you rewrite them?

6. Do you struggle with asking for help? What might it look like to accept support from someone safe this week?

7. In what ways have you tried to "fix" or "hold things together" for others? How has that shaped your identity?

8. What would a truly restful and safe night of sleep look and feel like for you? What steps can you take to move closer to that reality?

9. What parts of your story still feel unspoken or hidden? What might healing begin to look like in those places?

10. Who in your life helps you feel safe, grounded, and accepted as you are? How can you nurture those connections?

11. What are you grateful for today?

12. What is one action you can take today to show greater awareness, presence, or intention toward a healthier mindset?

Self–Sabotaging Behaviors and Coping Skills

CHAPTER SUMMARY

This chapter explores the root causes and manifestations of self-sabotaging behaviors—often born from early abandonment, emotional neglect, trauma, and disrupted attachment. The author reflects on her own coping mechanisms, including people-pleasing, procrastination, perfectionism, and hyper-independence.

As a child forced to self-soothe and parent herself (and her siblings), the author developed behaviors that initially helped her survive, but later sabotaged her relationships, trust, dreams, and even her health. Through powerful personal stories—like giving up her dream of being a news anchor due to fear of abandonment—she illustrates how past wounds shaped present patterns.

The chapter also emphasizes transformation: how self-awareness, support systems, faith, and intentional change can lead to healing. The journey isn't about blaming others but about breaking cycles and reclaiming agency.

KEY THEMES & INSIGHTS

- **Survival Coping Becomes Sabotage:** Early self-soothing or coping mechanisms often evolve into harmful adult behaviors.

- **The Illusion of Control:** Trying to control people or situations to prevent pain can lead to deeper dysfunction.

- **Distorted Identity:** Lack of secure attachment can lead to feelings of unworthiness and the need to perform for love.

- **Healing Through Awareness:** Naming and understanding self-sabotage is the first step toward healing.

- **Attachment Impacts Everything:** Early relationships shape our adult emotional responses and interactions.

- **Faith and Self-Compassion:** Truth, forgiveness, and grace are essential in reshaping a healthy identity.

JOURNAL QUESTIONS

1. What self-soothing habits did you develop as a child? Do they still show up in your adult life?

2. How has fear of abandonment shaped your choices in relationships or your career?

3. Have you ever given up a goal or dream out of fear of rejection, failure, or disapproval? What would it look like to revisit that dream?

4. What patterns do you see in your life that might be forms of self-sabotage (e.g., procrastination, perfectionism, shutting people out)?

5. What emotions or beliefs rise up when you try to trust others or let someone help you?

6. Do you relate to the idea of being the 'hero' child? How did that role affect your identity and expectations of yourself?

7. What are some "ungodly beliefs" or false narratives you have carried about your worth, abilities, or value?

8. What is one behavior or habit you want to shift from self-sabotage to self-support? What small step can you take this week?

9. What would it look like to treat yourself with the same love, patience, and encouragement you offer others?

10. How can you practice self-trust and faith in moments when old patterns try to take over?

11. What are you grateful for today?

12. What is one action you can take today to show greater awareness, presence, or intention toward a healthier mindset?

C H A P T E R   F I V E

Ignoring Appetites and Bodily Functions

CHAPTER SUMMARY

In this candid and emotionally layered chapter, the author explores how abandonment and emotional neglect can lead to the disconnection from one's own bodily needs—hunger, rest, elimination, and even self-awareness. From holding her bladder as a child because no one asked if she needed to go, to years of disordered eating, over-exercising, and ignoring hunger cues, the author paints a vivid picture of how trauma disrupts our most basic instincts.

She traces these patterns back to childhood experiences where her physical needs were unmet or even mocked. Over time, she learned to override her body's signals, seeking instead to control her environment through performance, perfectionism, and constant busyness. The chapter also highlights the physiological effects of trauma, referencing Dr. Bessel van der Kolk's *The Body Keeps the Score* to illustrate how trauma reshapes brain development and nervous system regulation.

Ultimately, the chapter offers hope. Through therapy, faith, self-compassion, and a willingness to listen to her body, the author has reclaimed ownership over her basic needs. She emphasizes the importance of recognizing that healing doesn't require perfection—just permission to listen, feel, and care for oneself with grace.

KEY THEMES & INSIGHTS

- **Disconnection from the Body:** Trauma causes us to ignore hunger, rest, or the need to use the bathroom.

- **Trauma Rewires the Brain:** Childhood trauma prioritizes survival over self-care.

- **Comparison and Body Shame:** Comparison leads to disordered eating and poor self-image.

- **Perfectionism and Performance:** Success masks wounds of rejection and invisibility.

- **Healing through Awareness:** Recognition of trauma symptoms is the first step to recovery.

- **Gratitude and Growth:** Gratitude becomes a path to peace and self-acceptance.

JOURNAL QUESTIONS

1. What bodily signals (like hunger, exhaustion, or needing to use the restroom) do you tend to ignore or suppress? Why?

2. What messages did you receive as a child about food, rest, or your body that still affect you today?

3. Have you ever experienced shame for simply having basic human needs? How does that impact your daily life now?

4. Think about the term "acceptance hunger." What kinds of approval or validation are you still chasing?

5. Do you see any perfectionist tendencies in yourself? How do those relate to your sense of safety or self-worth?

6. What's one small way you can begin to listen to your body more kindly and consistently?

7. In what ways have you been trying to protect yourself by controlling your food, appearance, or physical routines?

8. What do you need to hear today to believe that you are enough, just as you are? Write that affirmation down.

9. How do your eating or sleeping habits reflect past trauma or current stress? What could change if you gave yourself permission to rest or eat without guilt?

10. What does reclaiming your body and voice look like for you in this season of life?

11. What are you grateful for today?

12. What is one action you can take today to show greater awareness, presence, or intention toward a healthier mindset?

How Abandonment Affects Health

CHAPTER SUMMARY

This chapter explores how unresolved abandonment impacts the body, mind, and spirit. The author recounts years of living in survival mode—ignoring bodily signals, struggling with health issues like asthma, digestive problems, joint pain, and sleep disturbances, all linked to early emotional neglect and trauma. She shares personal anecdotes of dissociation, looping anxiety, and the physical consequences of stress and shame.

Over time, she discovered the deep connection between emotional wounds and chronic health conditions. Diagnosis brought relief, offering language and validation for lifelong struggles. Through therapy, faith, grounding techniques, and self-awareness, she began to heal and reframe her story—understanding that healing is a choice and a process. The chapter closes with an empowering reminder: health and wholeness are within reach, but require intentional effort and self-compassion.

KEY THEMES & INSIGHTS

- **The Body Remembers Trauma:** Chronic conditions like asthma, gut issues, joint pain, and fatigue often trace back to unresolved emotional wounds. Living in hypervigilance depletes the body and causes wear on major systems.

- **Emotional Health Is Physical Health:** Suppressed emotions manifest as physical pain, digestive distress, tension, and illness. Conditions like ADHD, CPTSD (Complex Post Traumatic Stress Disorder), and anxiety are often linked to childhood emotional neglect (CEN).

- **Dissociation as Survival:** Trauma can cause the brain to "check out" during high-stress moments, leading to memory gaps, emotional detachment, and missed bodily cues.

- **Shame vs. Guilt:** Guilt relates to behavior; shame targets identity. The shame from abandonment erodes self-worth and creates a cycle of avoidance and illness.

- **Healing Through Awareness and Practice:** Naming feelings, breathing techniques, grounding strategies, and therapy (like CBT and Reality Therapy) are powerful tools to retrain the brain and body.

- **The Choice to Heal:** Healing is not accidental—it requires responsibility, reflection, and vulnerability. Ignoring your story prolongs suffering; owning it reclaims your power and future.

JOURNAL QUESTIONS

1. What physical symptoms have you experienced that might be linked to unresolved emotional pain?

2. In what ways do you notice your body reacting during moments of high stress?

3. How do you typically respond when someone wants to discuss emotions with you?

4. When was the last time you dissociated or felt mentally "checked out"? What triggered it?

5. How do you distinguish between guilt and shame in your self-talk?

6. What are your current coping mechanisms when you're feeling overwhelmed? Are they helpful or harmful?

7. Have you ever ignored or minimized a physical issue because you thought it was "normal"?

8. How has abandonment affected your ability to sleep, eat, or breathe?

9. What are some grounding techniques that help you feel safe and present in your body?

10. What does it look like to take responsibility for your health—physically, emotionally, and spiritually?

11. How would your life change if you truly believed you were worthy of health and healing?

12. What support systems (people, therapies, resources) could you reach out to today?

13. What "small wins" have you experienced recently in managing stress or anxiety?

14. What past trauma are you ready to begin facing with grace and courage?

15. What new belief do you want to hold about yourself moving forward?

16. What are you grateful for today?

17. What is one action you can take today to show greater awareness, presence, or intention toward a healthier mindset?

How Abandonment Affects Wealth

CHAPTER SUMMARY

This chapter explores how childhood abandonment and trauma can deeply influence adult financial wellbeing. The author recounts personal experiences of self-sabotage, low self-worth, and fear rooted in early abandonment, which created a 'poverty mindset.' These inner wounds led to missed opportunities, undercharging for services, and constant fear of rejection.

She illustrates her healing journey—how stepping out in faith, embracing authenticity, and confronting abandonment-based beliefs brought not only emotional healing but also financial breakthrough. Through stories of personal growth, class experiences, and confrontations with limiting beliefs, she highlights how internal transformation led to external prosperity. The chapter ends with a call to embrace one's worth and originality to truly step into financial and personal abundance.

KEY THEMES & INSIGHTS

- **Abandonment Shapes Financial Identity:** Childhood experiences of being left or dismissed embed beliefs of unworthiness and expectations of failure. These beliefs unconsciously limit earning potential and confidence in seizing financial opportunities.

- **The Power of Internal Dialogue:** Negative self-talk driven by abandonment ('I am not worth it,' 'They don't really like me') stifles growth and connection. Healing starts by replacing those voices with truth and affirmations of worth.

- **Missed Opportunities Due to Fear:** The fear of rejection or failure keeps many from taking risks or accepting opportunities ('big table' moments). Success often begins with a decision to act in spite of fear.

- **Authenticity Increases Value:** People are drawn to what is real, not polished perfection. Vulnerability and truth-telling lead to deeper connections—and financial reward. Self-acceptance and showing up as your true self changes how others perceive and value you.

- **Healing is a Process, Not a Destination:** The journey involves setbacks, realizations, grace, and continued growth. Financial growth is tied to emotional healing and a shift in mindset.

JOURNAL QUESTIONS

1. What early experiences may have shaped your beliefs about money and self-worth?

2. Who abandoned you, and how has that shaped your sense of self-value?

3. What are some thoughts you repeatedly tell yourself about your capabilities or worth?

4. Where might these thoughts be coming from—and are they true?

5. What opportunity have you recently avoided due to fear or insecurity?

6. What might happen if you chose to act anyway?

7. In what areas of your life do you feel like you are "performing" rather than being authentic?

8. What does "being yourself" look like in those situations?

9. How have your emotions and past experiences impacted your income or financial decisions?

10. What healing step could you take today that might open the door to more abundance?

11. What are some ways you can affirm your worth daily?

12. How could you price or value your work differently now that you recognize your value?

13. Where in your life are you still "sitting at the kids' table"?

14. What would it look like to take your place at the 'big table' now?

15. What are you grateful for today?

16. What is one action you can take today to show greater awareness, presence, or intention toward a healthier mindset?

How Abandonment Affects Relationships

CHAPTER SUMMARY

Chapter Eight delves into the profound and often invisible ways abandonment impacts our ability to form and maintain relationships. Dr. Rena Perozich weaves together personal experiences, generational trauma, and research-based insights to explore how abandonment can create trust issues, co-dependency, low self-esteem, and an inability to set healthy boundaries. She identifies how childhood family roles shape adult behavior and describes how healing is possible through awareness, therapy, healthy boundaries, and spiritual growth. The chapter closes with hope: though the past cannot be changed, the future can be shaped through intentional relationship work.

KEY THEMES AND INSIGHTS

- **Generational Trauma and Patterns:** Abandonment issues can be passed down over generations and manifest in behaviors and emotional responses.

- **Trust and Intimacy Struggles:** Abandonment often breeds deep-seated trust issues and the fear of emotional vulnerability.

- **Identity and Role Confusion:** Children in dysfunctional families often assume survival roles (e.g., Responsible Child, Placater) that carry into adult relationships.

- **Boundaries and Co-Dependency:** A lack of clear boundaries leads to over-responsibility, burnout, and relational dysfunction.

- **Emotional Awareness and Healing:** Developing emotional literacy and healing the wounded inner child allows for more authentic relationships.

- **The Power of Healthy Relationships:** Relationships are essential to human well-being. Healing often begins in safe, nurturing connections.

JOURNAL QUESTIONS

Understanding the Past

1. What abandonment experiences—direct or generational—have shaped how you view relationships?

2. Can you identify patterns of abandonment in your family history? How have they affected your behavior or emotions?

Self-Awareness in Relationships

3. How do you typically respond to trust and closeness? Do you pull back, people-please, or overcompensate?

4. Which childhood role do you most identify with (Responsible Child, Placater, Adjuster, Acting Out Child)?

Boundaries and Identity

5. Where in your life do you struggle with setting or maintaining boundaries?

6. What small step could you take today to honor your needs in a relationsh p without guilt or fear?

Healing and Growth

7. Who are the safe people in your life that support your growth and healing?

8. What does a healthy, interdependent relationship look like to you?

Forgiveness and Freedom

9. Is there someone you need to forgive (yourself or others) to break free from the cycle of abandonment?

10. What belief about yourself or others are you willing to release so you can experience healing in your relationships?

11. What are you grateful for today?

12. What is one action you can take today to show greater awareness, presence, or intention toward a healthier mindset?

The Fear of Loss and Disappointments

CHAPTER SUMMARY

In this deeply personal and emotionally raw chapter, Dr. Rena Perozich explores the lifelong emotional impact of loss and disappointment through the lens of abandonment. Drawing from her own experiences—losing her infant daughter, her younger brother, her home in a fire, and enduring parental abandonment—she reveals how unprocessed grief and early emotional neglect shape identity and behaviors.

She weaves together personal narrative, scripture (specifically the story of Job), psychology, and observations from literature to illuminate how early abandonment intensifies the fear of future loss. The chapter also touches on coping mechanisms such as overachievement, perfectionism, and emotional detachment. Ultimately, Dr. Perozich shares how embracing vulnerability and learning to 'be present' with loved ones and her Savior have brought healing and growth.

KEY THEMES AND INSIGHTS

- **Abandonment Intensifies Grief:** Losses are more deeply felt when compounded by unresolved childhood abandonment. Grief becomes overwhelming and identity-shaping.

- **Unprocessed Trauma Repeats in Patterns:** Dr. Perozich demonstrates how abandonment, left unhealed, leads to self-sabotaging behaviors in relationships and a cycle of expectation and disappointment.

- **Grief Beyond Death:** Grieving someone doesn't require their death. Emotional absence, abandonment, and even the failure of expected events can evoke deep mourning.

- **Desire for Closure:** The longing for final words like "Love you, bye" illustrates the need for closure and acknowledgment in relationships—often unmet in early life.

- **Perfectionism as a Mask:** Overachievement and control (e.g., through appearance or performance) become ways to hide inner pain and unworthiness.

- **Healing Through Presence and Connection:** True healing begins with being emotionally present—with oneself, others, and their Creator.

- **Faith and Spiritual Reflection:** Scripture and spiritual reflection serve as a source of comfort, insight, and strength throughout her grieving and healing process.

JOURNAL QUESTIONS

1. What is one loss (of a person, place, or expectation) that shaped your life significantly? How did it affect your sense of identity?

2. Can you recall a time when disappointment felt larger than the event itself? Do you think past experiences may have intensified your reaction?

3. What are some ways you try to control your environment to avoid feeling vulnerable? How might these behaviors relate to deeper fears?

4. In what ways have early experiences of emotional neglect or abandonment affected how you form (or avoid) relationships today?

5. Are there any relationships or situations where you never received closure? What would you want to say or hear if you had the chance?

6. What would doing things differently look like for you today—in how you love, parent, relate, or care for yourself?

7. What are ways you can be more emotionally present with people you love this week? What might you need to let go of to do that?

8. How does your faith or spirituality support you in times of loss or fear? Are there scriptures, prayers, or practices that ground you?

9. What are you grateful for today?

10. What is one action you can take today to show greater awareness, presence, or intention toward a healthier mindset?

C H A P T E R   T E N

The Fear of Intimacy

CHAPTER SUMMARY

In this heartfelt and revealing chapter, Dr. Rena Perozich confronts the complex relationship between intimacy and abandonment. Drawing from her personal experiences, attachment theory, and psychological research, she uncovers how fear of intimacy stems from early childhood emotional neglect (CEN), abandonment, and abuse. Rather than embracing closeness, those with abandonment wounds often resist vulnerability, fearing exposure and rejection

The chapter breaks down the four attachment styles—avoidant, ambivalent, disorganized, and secure—highlighting how each responds to intimacy. Through reflection, the author exposes her own avoidant and ambivalent behaviors, shaped by trauma, control, and distrust. She candidly discusses her dissociation, "TMI" oversharing, perfectionism, and deep longing to be seen and loved.

Ultimately, Dr. Perozich shows that healing from abandonment and developing healthy intimacy is possible through awareness, support, emotional presence, and courage. She encourages readers to reject false core beliefs and embrace relationships marked by empathy, safety, and love.

KEY THEMES AND INSIGHTS

- **Intimacy is More than Physical:** True intimacy involves emotional, intellectual, experiential, and spiritual connection, not just sex. It requires vulnerability and trust.

- **Attachment Styles Shape Intimacy:** Avoidant, ambivalent, disorganized, and secure attachment styles deeply affect one's capacity for closeness and relationship satisfaction.

- **Avoidant Behaviors Mask Pain:** People with avoidant attachment style often avoid disclosure, nonsexual touch, and emotional closeness due to fear of being hurt again.

- **Childhood Emotional Neglect (CEN) Distorts Self-Perception:** CEN leads to dissociation, low self-worth, perfectionism, and difficulty receiving love, all of which undermine intimacy.

- **Healing Requires Rewiring Core Beliefs:** Deeply rooted beliefs like "I am not worthy" must be replaced with truth. You are worthy of love and capable of intimacy.

- **Emotional Presence is Key:** Being present and grounded in relationships helps to build trust, especially for those who dissociate or emotionally withdraw under stress.

- **Recovering from Co-dependency:** Learning to set boundaries, expect respect, and stop over-functioning in relationships are vital steps toward healing.

- **Trusting Others and Self Again:** Even abandoned individuals can build healthy relationships by recognizing their worth and slowly letting trustworthy people in.

JOURNAL QUESTIONS

1. What does intimacy mean to you beyond physical closeness? How comfortable are you with emotional or spiritual intimacy?

2. Which attachment style do you most identify with—avoidant, ambivalent, disorganized, or secure? How does that affect your relationships?

3. Can you recall a time when you recoiled from closeness or sharing your true self? What were you afraid would happen?

4. What are some core beliefs you hold about yourself in relationships? Are they rooted in truth or old wounds?

5. How do you respond when someone tries to get emotionally close to you? What feelings come up in those moments?

6. Do you recognize any patterns of over-sharing or avoiding emotional intimacy in your life? Why might these patterns have developed?

7. What childhood messages did you receive about emotions, trust, or connection? How have they shaped your adult relationships?

THE BLUE JEAN JACKET

8. What does a healthy, safe, and loving relationship look like to you today? What small steps can you take to cultivate more intimacy in your life?

9. What are you grateful for today?

10. What is one action you can take today to show greater awareness, presence, or intention toward a healthier mindset?

Dissociation

CHAPTER SUMMARY

In Chapter 11, Dr. Rena Perozich offers a vulnerable and powerful account of her personal experiences with dissociation, a defense mechanism she developed as a response to childhood emotional neglect, abandonment, and undiagnosed trauma. She recounts the disorienting memory lapses, emotional detachment, and episodes where she functioned without fully being present—physically there but emotionally absent.

Her dissociation, often misread as forgetfulness or irresponsibility, was later understood as a symptom of Complex PTSD and alexithymia—an inability to identify and describe emotions. She examines how her unresolved wounds disrupted not just her internal world but also her relationships, including with her children. Through self-awareness, boundaries, and grounding practices, she is learning to remain present, regulate her emotions, and repair the generational cycle of abandonment and emotional absence.

Dr. Perozich concludes with a message of hope: healing is possible when we acknowledge our wounds, confront our patterns, and commit to showing up—fully present—for ourselves and those we love.

KEY THEMES AND INSIGHTS

- **Dissociation as a Coping Mechanism:** Dissociation can manifest as memory loss, emotional detachment, or "going through the motions" in order to survive overwhelming feelings or trauma.

- **Complex PTSD and Emotional Neglect:** Childhood abandonment and emotional neglect can lead to lifelong struggles with trust, presence, memory, and emotional regulation.

- **The Impact of Unhealed Trauma on Parenting:** Unaddressed trauma often leads to performance-based parenting and emotional unavailability, repeating generational cycles.

- **Alexithymia and Emotional Blindness:** Difficulty identifying and expressing emotions is common in trauma survivors and often leads to internal confusion and relational disconnection.

- **The Importance of Presence Over Perfection:** Healing begins when we prioritize being emotionally present rather than striving to be flawless or hyperproductive.

- **Setting Boundaries and Grounding Techniques:** Awareness of limitations, using sensory grounding, and creating systems for support (like reminders and clear communication) are essential for staying present.

- **Breaking Generational Patterns:** Through honesty, apology, and effort to connect emotionally, it is possible to stop passing on patterns of abandonment to future generations.

- **Freedom through Self-Awareness and Acceptance:** Naming and understanding dissociation is the first step toward reclaiming agency, peace, and connection in one's life.

JOURNAL QUESTIONS

1. Have you ever experienced "zoning out" or memory lapses during emotional or stressful events? What might have triggered those moments?

2. How do you typically respond to emotional discomfort—do you lean in, withdraw, or dissociate?

3. Were emotional needs acknowledged or dismissed in your childhood? How has that shaped your ability to identify and express emotions now?

4. What does emotional presence mean to you? In which relationships do you find it hardest to remain emotionally present?

5. Reflect on your parenting or caregiving—how do you think your past experiences may have influenced how you show up emotionally?

6. What grounding practices or tools could help you stay emotionally and physically present in overwhelming situations?

7. What are some internal narratives or beliefs you hold that might be rooted in past abandonment or trauma?

8. What would healing look like for you today if you were to choose presence over performance?

9. What are you grateful for today?

10. What is one action you can take today to show greater awareness, presence, or intention toward a healthier mindset?

Wearing a New Jacket

CHAPTER SUMMARY

Chapter 12 is a deeply personal and hopeful conclusion to the author's healing journey. Rena reflects on her restored relationship with her mother—an emotional milestone marked by an unexpected apology. While the apology did not erase past pain, it validated her experiences and offered a sense of peace and freedom. Rena also acknowledges the unwavering support of her husband throughout her healing, and how his presence helped stabilize her in the midst of emotional turmoil.

She explores the transformational power of personal change and forgiveness. The chapter emphasizes that healing does not rely on others changing but starts with in oneself. It also encourages the reader to embrace vulnerability, seek coaching or mentorship, and to share their stories to foster community and healing in others.

In closing, the "new jacket" symbolizes her internal transformation—confidence, wholeness, and peace that radiate outward, even if not visibly seen.

KEY THEMES AND INSIGHTS

- **Healing Through Validation and Forgiveness:** An apology, while not a solution to the past, offers validation and a critical moment of healing.

- **Transformation Through Relationship and Support:** The consistent support of her husband represents the stabilizing power of love and safe relationships.

- **The Journey of Self-Awareness and Rewriting the Narrative:** Emotional recovery is a personal journey—progressive and uneven, but ultimately empowering.

- **Empowerment Through Coaching and Community:** Seeking mentorship or coaching can be a turning point in one's healing.

- **Letting Go of the Past to Embrace the Future:** It's okay to remember the past, but the future holds greater promise.

JOURNAL QUESTIONS

1. What does forgiveness mean to you personally? Is there someone you need to forgive—even without an apology?

2. What would your own "new jacket" look like? What changes in you are invisible to others but deeply felt within?

3. Who has been your "eye of the storm"? How have they helped you through your healing process?

4. What part of your story are you ready to rewrite? How can you begin doing that today?

5. How do you want your story to impact others? What would it mean for your healing to help someone else begin theirs?

6. What does it look like for you to visit the past without living there? What steps can you take to move more confidently into your future?

7. What are you grateful for today?

8. What is one action you can take today to show greater awareness, presence, or intention toward a healthier mindset?

A B O U T   T H E   A U T H O R

Dr. Rena Perozich

Apassionate pastor, author, and global speaker whose prophetic ministry and healing anointing have impacted lives in over 20 nations. A native of West Virginia, she is the founder and host of Women of Witness, a mult -denominational women's ministry that equips and encourages women to find their God-given purpose and cultivate strong, Christ-centered relationships.

Rena hosts *The Answer to Your Prayers,* a global shortwave radio program on Hope Radio with a reach of 3.7 billion listeners. You can tune in by visiting *HopeRadio.net.* She also serves as Senior Elder at Restoration Church International and is ordained through MFC Ministries.

As a mentor and pastoral counselor, Rena is known for her wisdom, prophetic insight, and heart for people. Her books, *The ABCs of Being a Mother, Moments that Matter, Don't Fear FIGHT, The Blue Jean Jacket,* and *The Blue Jean Jacket Reflection Journal* are available on Amazon. In addition to these publications, she is also the author of *Love & Marriage,* a magazine column published bi-monthly.

Rena maintains an active presence on social media, where she shares biblical encouragement, teachings, and inspiration for women of faith. She also co-hosts *Believe Right,* a weekly television program aired regionally and online, alongside her husband, Joe.

Learn more at
renaperozich.com